States of Consciousness

VOLUME II

Reflections

Rasul H. Muhammad

States of Consciousness - Volume II - Reflections

Copyright 2016 Rasul H. Muhammad
All Rights Reserved under International Copyright Law.
Contents and/or cover may not be reproduced in whole or
in part in any form without written consent of the author.

Publisher: G.C. Productions Group, Inc. (Chicago, IL)
Editor/Designer: Modern Maryam, LLC (New York, NY)

ISBN-13: 978-0-9982183-0-4
ISBN-10: 0-9982183-0-8

Printed in the United States of America.

Ever since I could walk, I can remember awakening to hear the sound of the typewriter. It was my Mother, typing and typing her many inspirational thoughts, or maybe a column for the Muhammad Speaks newspaper. I cannot recall a single moment in conversation with my Mother where she was not sharing with me the Teachings of my Father, the Most Honorable Elijah Muhammad. Everything I do, with the help and guidance of Almighty God Allah, will be done in honor of this extraordinary woman, my Mom,
Mother Tynnetta Muhammad,
whose life is still unfolding.

TABLE OF CONTENTS

About the Author	iii
Foreward	v
Introduction	viii
Author's Preface	xii
On Life & Living	1
Developing My Relationship with Allah	15
The Great Jihad: The Struggle Within	37
Dis-Ease & Healing	83
Life, Love & Relationships	109
God & Religion	145
The Time	185
Concluding Thoughts	201
Epilogue	213
Acknowledgements	216

States of Consciousness

ABOUT THE AUTHOR

Rasul H. Muhammad is a son of the Most Honorable Elijah Muhammad and Mother Tynnetta Muhammad. He is a Student Minister in the Nation of Islam, under the leadership of the Honorable Minister Louis Farrakhan.

Commissioned by Minister Farrakhan in 2015 to vanguard the Ministry of Love, Brother Rasul is currently on tour sharing a divine message of love and healing throughout the Nation. As The Honorable Minister Louis Farrakhan has said, "The Ministry of Love is a Ministry of Healing." This is proving true as individuals around the world are bearing witness to the impactful power of unconditional love that they experience through the Ministry of Love, including healing spiritual and physical healing.

An accomplished singer, songwriter, producer, and performance artist, Brother Rasul is using these gifts now in his capacity as a Student Minister in the Ministry of Love. Follow him and the Ministry of Love on social media today.

Twitter | @BrotherRasul
Facebook | rasul.muhammad.3
Email | gcproductionsgroupinc@gmail.com

States of Consciousness

FOREWARD

Allah's LOVE is Healing, and comes to us through individuals. The Ministry of Love is a Ministry of Healing, and promises to deliver such to all who will receive its message that is coming through the vessel of a man who has suffered and presently continues to suffer great physical pain and serious health challenges on a daily basis. What seems to have qualified him to be such a messenger, is the same test that each of us face: What is our attitude in the face of trial? In the experience of pain? In the midst of opposition? Our response in attitude and behavior determines whether each of us, individually, may similarly qualify ourselves to carry and share with others a divine light and love that is healing, medicinal and transformative, the source of which is none other than the One God, Allah, from whom we were all created and by whose permission we all are permitted to exist, endure, and evolve.

Commissioned by the Honorable Minister Louis Farrakhan to vanguard The Ministry of Love in the Nation of Islam, this appointment has given Brother Rasul a new sense of purpose in life. As a legally blind man diagnosed with kidney failure, he faces serious health issues that require he undergo dialysis treatment three times a week. His passion to help the Honorable Minister Louis Farrakhan, whom he affectionately refers to as his "Tio" (or Uncle in Spanish), and his passion to serve the people of God, has driven him to travel across the Nation despite his personal condition, working beyond fatigue day after day, city after city, seemingly pausing only to visit a local dialysis center to receive treatment . . . all done for the sake of Allah, that he can continue to share with the Believers what Allah is inspiring in him.

This book is the second volume in a mini-series compiling ideas and thoughts that have come through Brother Rasul's personal reflection of his individual experience during a unique time in his life. Nearly one year ago, Brother Rasul shared with the world from the rostrum of Mosque Maryam, in Chicago, his personal experience with hitting 'rock bottom', and the moment when Allah's LOVE saved him from suicide. While in the process of literally taking steps to end his own life, he was interupted when a close family member called him and asked, "Do you know that Allah loves you?" From this simple question came the most profound realization, that not only does Allah love us all, but "He loves me, *individually* . . . Allah loves *me*, INDIVIDUALLY!" From this one, powerful thought, Brother Rasul has been feeding, healing, and evolving ever since.

This is the love that heals - Allah's Love. And Allah's love for each of us, individually, comes to us, through people. Since he was commissioned by the Honorable Minister Louis

Foreward

Farrakhan to vanguard the Ministry of Love, which ultimately must become part of every other Ministry there is, Brother Rasul has worked tirelessly to share this message with all who would be open to listen. When cities invite him, he gives of himself through the ministry working non-stop with focus on benefiting the Believers, often to the neglect of his own condition. In between tour dates, Brother Rasul unremittingly shares with the Believers, and all who will listen, as host of a weekly live chat show, as well as the regular commentator on the Fajr Prayer Line every Wednesday morning. Through it all, it is clearly apparent to any who hears or beholds him that the most important thing and one in his life, is ALLAH, God. His love for Allah is the driving force in all that he does. His daily activity and sacrifices, are all for his love of Him. And out of his love for Allah, he has love for His Beloved, the People of God. This, perhaps, is the key ingredient enabling the result of those who experience the Ministry of Love bearing witness to its divine effect. Unconditional LOVE is the channel through which healing is coming forth.

Vivian X Lee
Editor/Designer

INTRODUCTION

I was asked just a few days before the publishing of this book, by my beautiful brother and friend, Rasul, to write something that would be included in his wonderfully revealing testimony. I truly consider this to be a great honor and I am deeply humbled.

Dear Reader,

Every human being is a *gifted* **gift** from Allah (God). Every human being has the potential to fulfill the Will of the Creator and accomplish the goal of life. We are all born of purpose.

A gift is something that someone generally receives that has to be unwrapped and unpackaged to reveal the value of its contents. The gift cannot unwrap itself, so, **how do we unwrap ourselves?**

The Holy Quran teaches us that Allah ordained struggle for each of us.

My dear and beloved teacher, the Honorable Minister

Introduction

Louis Farrakhan, said, "Allah created the human being to struggle and to face difficulties. It is only when you struggle, it is only when you face the difficulties of your life, that it brings out of you what the Creator put in you."

No life that comes into the world comes into existence without struggle and pain. The struggle and pain that is associated with life tells us something about its tremendous value. The little bird is seen struggling pecking its way out of the egg. Then the little bird struggles to get its balance to fly, but once it flies, it is gone. A child develops and struggles in the womb of the mother, and when it is time to come forth, the mother goes through labor pains to bring forth the new life. Both the mother and the child experience pain, and the pain that was associated with that struggle to be born leaves a sign in a bruise or birth mark.

The Honorable Minister Louis Farrakhan taught me that pain brings to birth new realities, and that nothing new comes into existence without pain, struggle, and sacrifice, and no servant comes to God except that he or she is tried.

I have had the great blessing of watching my brother's growth and evolutionary development to be a servant of Allah and a helper in the Messianic Work and Mission of his Father. I have personally witnessed his many trials, his ups and downs, his heartaches and pains, to his joys and moments of happiness. It has truly been a humbling and rewarding experience.

States of Consciousness

In Rasul's trials, he has discovered something so wonderfully amazing and liberating that everyone needs to know it, and that is . . . **Allah is God and Allah Loves YOU!**

Rasul is a *gifted* **gift** from Allah who has been on a journey to ***know*** the certainty of Allah's (God's) presence in our lives. Allah has been with each of us from the very beginning when we were, each, a single cell. All of our lives, we seek acceptance, validation and security. The problem for most, however, is that we have been looking in the wrong places. The peace, validation and security we seek in life come from the knowledge of God and knowing that He is ever-present in our lives.

As we read this book, we will learn aspects of ourselves through the prism of the writer's life, as we all struggle for balance to be in harmony in accord with Allah (God). Harmony with Allah (God) manifests the gifts in us and reveals the immeasurable value of our lives. Rasul's thoughts and reflections in this book represent what he has discovered of Allah's Majestic Will.

Of Rasul's many life trials taking him to the door of despair, hopelessness and even to near death, Rasul comes back to tell the living that there is hope and life worthy to live.

May the reader be enlightened, strengthened and encouraged. May this book help in the unwrapping of you and me, the *gifted* **gifts**, to be put into the service of Allah

Introduction

(God) for the upliftment of humanity in the establishment of the Kingdom of Heaven.

> "And now these three remain: faith, hope and love. But the greatest of these is Love."

Ishmael R. Muhammad
National Assistant to the Hon. Minister Louis Farrakhan
September 28, 2016

AUTHOR'S PREFACE

My grand-nephew Imam Sultan Rahman Muhammad, the Nation of Islam's first Imam from the Teachings of the Most Honorable Elijah Muhammad, taught me the following from the sayings of Prophet Muhammad (PBUH): The language of Arabic, thought of as a national language for the Arab people and hence the chosen language through which the Holy Quran was revealed, is actually *in* the tongue.

While it is true that Arabic is the oldest language spoken by the original people of the earth when our planet was found, it is not and must not be thought of as a national language. Prophet Muhammad (PBUH) reportedly said that "Arabic is *in* the tongue." This would mean that the mathematical expression and constitution of the language itself is deeper than the climatic conditions that influence its many dialects, as in the case of all major languages. *Arabic is in the tongue because the word itself is in the nature of the original human being,* created to be upright in the obedience to ALLAH (GOD).

Author's Preface

My father, the Most Honorable Elijah Muhammad taught us that Arabia is in the Far East and is bordered by the Indian Ocean on the south. There are many sub-languages spoken by different groups in all of these areas. What is deeper than the tongue, as a means by which the human being communicated most effectively . . . ? The answer, is, LOVE.

The Most Honorable Elijah Muhammad taught that LOVE is the building block of the entire universe of ALLAH'S creation. LOVE is life itself! LOVE is GOD! LOVE is the original nature of all organic forms! All spoken languages of the people of modern day Earth are but dialects, at best, of LOVE. LOVE is the source and inspiration of this book. Therefore, I suspect, healing will be the experience of the reader. Enjoy!

Rasul H. Muhammad
September 30, 2016

States of Consciousness

On Life & Living

States of Consciousness

ENJOYING life is not the aim of life.

Enjoying life is the result of living life for the Glory of GOD.

THE aim of life is not simply to be enjoyed, but to be LIVED in *obedience* to the Will and Way of ALLAH (GOD)!

Anything else is not living life to the fullest.

On Life & Living

WHAT is Success in this Life?

Success in this life is when your FAITH and TRUST in
ALLAH (GOD/DIOS), and His Promise, enables you to resist
the satanic TEMPTATIONS of this world's money,
material wealth, and its women.
Let not these things excite you . . .
The promise of ALLAH is so much greater still!

States of Consciousness

---

*S*UCCESS or failure in life is in-direct proportion to the *attitude* we choose before a trial. Keep in mind, that the remembrance of ALLAH (GOD/DIOS) is the *greatest force*!

Your ATTITUDE will determine your ALTITUDE! ALLAH blesses those who PRAISE Him much!

SATAN is a great deceiver. He is not limited to color or race. Satan is a mindset.

Satan's ultimate aim is to disconnect us from our Divinity, from within. I think we must be very aware of this fact if we are 'Believers' in ALLAH and student-practitioners of the Teachings.
To the question of who is causing the trials in one's life, the Holy Qur'an says:
"Nothing befalls man other than what man's own hand has caused"
and
"Nothing happens without ALLAH's permission."

Which of these two would you grant the greater relative importance to the trials that befall us in life?

States of Consciousness

We, in our current state of consciousness, no longer reflect or represent GOD, His Truth, and His LOVE. We rebelled against our original nature and are now living a beast life. We are all but crawling around on all fours! We have truly gone astray. So, we have all become, to a degree, disbelievers and hypocrites to GOD in religion as we superstitiously, in the deep recess of our thinking, blame ALLAH (GOD / DIOS) for our condition.

It is our internal attitudes toward ALLAH
that MUST change,
if we are to be
saved,
healed,
and delivered.

Nothing has befallen us other than what our own thoughts and actions have caused.

States of Consciousness

We cause our own storms in life.

We must NEVER blame GOD or others for
our trials and misfortunes as if we are
innocent victims of circumstance or of
a 'devil' outside of OURSELVES!

We must study what we have done
within and *to* ourselves
to cause our own conditions.

Knowledge of this truth will set us FREE!

ONE day, the Minister said to me,
*"Son, I listen for GOD, in
everything and everyone."*

My after-thought was, "Wow!" How humble must the Minister, or anyone, BE, to think so little of themselves that they might detect GOD in *everything*. And how least in importance must we think of ourselves to listen for GOD in others no matter how different or
opposed to our ideas
they might be?

States of Consciousness

*L*OVE is the divine passcode to
all living creatures.

To love unconditionally is to
represent GOD!

On Life & Living

States of Consciousness

Developing My Relationship with Allah

States of Consciousness

We are not naturally or automatically
connected to GOD in our conscious minds
because we have been given,
by ALLAH, authority
over our own
'WILL'.

States of Consciousness

REFLECTIVE Questions for the BELIEVER in ALLAH (GOD / JEHOVAH / DIOS / THE CREATOR)

Do you LOVE ALLAH (GOD / DIOS) . . .
more than your children?

Do you LOVE Him . . .
more than your money and wealth?

Do you LOVE Him . . .
more than your own life?

Do you LOVE ALLAH (GOD) . . . *consciously?*

Do the people around you . . .
know that you LOVE GOD?

How do you *make GOD a part of your everyday?*

How is HE *in your relationships?*

> Do you think your LOVE relationship with GOD should be kept private and personal?

> In ISLAM, the 'believer' is taught that ALLAH blesses those who praise Him!

To disbelieve in Allah, is to disconnect from His Spirit.

To disconnect from Allah's Spirit is to die in mind, and ultimately, in body. Reconnection with ALLAH (GOD) is a matter of *humble repentance*.

States of Consciousness

WE, the 'Believers' in ALLAH (GOD), are so blessed that when experiencing anxiety, grief, lack of strength, laziness, cowardice and stinginess, being overpowered by debt and the oppressions of men, we only need to seek refuge in Our Lord and Saviour ALLAH to keep us away from what is prohibited and 'CLEAR' us of what is beside HIM.

To the Believers in GOD: We are truly blessed, and *by our prayers*, Highly Favored.

A MANTRA for the WISE and the HUMBLE:

Less of 'me', and more of ALLAH!

This is the 'Path' to infinite POWER!

States of Consciousness

MAN, as a finite form, cannot equal himself to GOD. He can only reflect GOD through his *infinite spirit*.
Worship GOD in spirit, not in form!

Developing My Relationship with Allah

HUMILITY of heart, mind and attitude makes us eligible to be used by ALLAH (GOD) and His Messenger. The opposite makes your character a vessel for Satan. When our connection with GOD is weak, PRIDE appears strong as a smoke-screen tor a fragile character. Fragility perceives any critique as an assault. PRIDE can't stand trial, but HUMILITY is grateful to correction.

BEING HUMBLE is a position of great *strength* and an *immunity* against PRIDE.

States of Consciousness

*H*UMILITY is the disposition that makes us *telepathatic* to God.

MAN has, to a degree, all of the attributes of God. This is how we are made in His Likeness. But without Love, we simply cannot reflect HIM!

States of Consciousness

NEVER underestimate the active participation of ALLAH (GOD) in present time, in your life, INDIVIDUALLY!

ALLAH is Lord of all the worlds!

I love ALLAH! He is my IMMUNITY.
He makes my enemies into my friends who help develop my character.

I Love ALLAH!

He is my Best Friend!

States of Consciousness

SATAN cannot influence you when you are in love with ALLAH!

The act of loving Allah creates a protective forcefield around your being!

WHEN a man loves and fears GOD,
his character is humble,
his way is respectful of everyone, and
his expression is MEASURED.

To Love and Fear ALLAH (GOD) purifies and dignifies the human being!

A Believer isn't just blessed.

A Believer is favored by Allah.

In HUMILITY, coupled with good conduct and respect for all, make the following your mantra for the day:

"ALLAH is not displeased with me . . . I AM HIS!"

States of Consciousness

WE, as Students of the Teachings of the Most Honorable Elijah Muhammad, must be careful not to generalize this most critical concept of ALLAH (GOD) appearing in the person of a 'Man'.

Man, in the English language, means a human being, regardless of sex/gender. However, men are not women anymore than women are men, yet ALLAH created both male and female of a single 'essence', so teaches the Holy Qur'an. ALLAH (GOD) is the 'ESSENCE'! We are not the equal of our CREATOR, yet we are Created to reflect and represent Him and all of His Righteousness through this finite form that must NEVER be worshiped or praised as GOD. Why? Because we as human beings in this finite organic form can only *reflect* the Infinite, but we in this form cannot *be* the INFINITE.

The Holy Qur'an says:
"*Say He ALLAH is One. ALLAH is He on Whom nothing is independent but upon Whom we all depend. He neither begets, nor is He begotten, and there is none like Him!*"

Developing My Relationship with Allah

WE have the potential of GOD's very nature, which is the nature out of which we were created in the beginning, being 'Upright', but we are *not* His equal in this finite form.

The Bible says: "Ye are all gods, children of the most High GOD." 'Children' here means immature and underdeveloped. We are no more gods than children are independent adults!

We NEED ALLAH's guidance through every stage of our development.
We NEED His MERCY for all the foolish mistakes we continue to make!

We NEED His PROTECTION against the consequences of our own misguided thoughts and behavior!

When we surrender in true humility to ALLAH, we will grow to channel His LOVE unconditionally!

GOD, is LOVE, and LOVE, is LIFE!
And these three being One, makes 'YOU'!

States of Consciousness

Faith in ALLAH (GOD) comes after
everything else
has failed.

Stop making GOD your last resort, and
make HIM your First Choice!

States of Consciousness

~ The Great Jihad ~
The Struggle Within

States of Consciousness

The Great Jihad

PAUL is recognized as the greatest of the Disciples of JESUS CHRIST. This morning, while in reflection of his discovery that we fight not against flesh and blood, but against SPIRITUAL WICKEDNESS, it occurred to me that Paul was not identifying an enemy in the government or rulership at the time.
Instead, he was identifying the
ENEMY WITHIN.

WICKEDNESS, according to theologians and philosophers, is a synonym for 'evil', which denotes the quality of a person's heart, mind or being. When PAUL is speaking of 'spiritual wickedness', he is speaking of the transgressions of his *own mind.*

States of Consciousness

*I*MAGINE yourself as the battlefield over which GOD and SATAN fight for Control. Which one will YOU allow to take control of *your* LIFE?

The Great Jihad

WHY wouldn't you want to clean up and make a way for GOD to reside within you?

Has Satan grown dominant in your character?

States of Consciousness

IN order for one to spiritually purify him or herself, they must first seek refuge in
Allah
(GOD/DIOS).

GOD is the Best Purifier!

THE 'inner-self' is subject to
CULTIVATION because
ALLAH (GOD) gave us free-will.
When the 'inner-self', or 'ego', is regimented by
moral discipline, it can evolve into the likeness of
its source . . .
GOD.

States of Consciousness

WITHOUT spiritual cultivation, our egos become material based. This conditioning compels the habit of judging everything and everyone as separate and unequal with a 'capitalistic' view that will always lack the element of human compassion, care and spiritual sensitivity.

The Great Jihad

*D*IVINE means that which comes directly from ALLAH (GOD). So, a divine trial is a reality, administered by GOD Himself, to manifest what is deep within us. The Holy Qur'an raises the reflective question, *"Do men think they will be left alone on saying they believe and not be tried?"*

We *all* must be tried.

States of Consciousness

THE spiritual, mental and physical purification process, better known as 'trials', are meant to help us overcome inordinate 'PRIDE'. Inordinate 'PRIDE' is when we think too much of ourselves and too little of the other person or the bigger picture.

The Human 'ego' is a 'god' in you that MUST be made submissive to the Supreme Being (GOD), in order to keep it from becoming your Devil.

The Great Jihad

We are in the time of UNIVERSAL CHANGE.

This means EVERYTHING and EVERYONE!

I read the words of a wise Asian man some years ago who wrote: "Maintaining status quo is regression."

Internal dissatisfaction is the impetus of change! Behold, ALLAH (GOD), the CREATOR, is making ALL things *new*. HE DEMANDS OF EVERY LIVING CREATURE!

Our Beloved Minister Louis Farrakhan teaches us that "Time dictates the agenda!"

States of Consciousness

THE severity of a 'trial' could indicate that ALLAH is reconstituting you for greater use in His 'Cause'. We are in a time period where nothing is as it appears because ALL are under trial.

WHEN ALLAH (GOD) wants to use 'YOU' to serve a particular purpose in life, He prepares you by trials that develop in you greater PATIENCE.

LOVE IS PATIENT.

States of Consciousness

SHAME and 'Guilt' are the
Friends of Change.

They are NOT our perceived 'enemies', but rather,
they are our friends. The human character in relation
to others does not mature until it experiences the
consequences of its own doing. When we are honest
enough with ourselves by acknowledging the incomplete
state that we are currently in, whereby we make
mistakes and errors, 'shame' and 'guilt'
become the agents of CHANGE.

CORRECTION and guidance are beautiful
if you are humble, and NOT bitter,
through disappointment.

With ALLAH's Help and Mercy,
we can get back on course,
and maybe,
get it right next time . . .
Insha-ALLAH!

States of Consciousness

*L*EARN to appreciate our moments of disappointment without becoming bitter. If you allow yourself to become bitter in disappointment, you may miss ALLAH's Grace in the exact moment when you lack understanding.

DISAPPOINTMENT is when what we hope for, expect or anticipate does not come to pass when we expect, or at all. The BLESSING to self is one of CORRECTIVE GUIDANCE because disappointment, no matter how big or small, is an indication that my will and way was not in sync with GOD's Will and Way.

The Great Jihad

*E*VEN in my disappointments,
   I can acquire great wisdom.

I'm so blessed, I dare not complain.

States of Consciousness

DISAPPOINTMENT is only a trial meant to test the worthiness of our character to receive all that He, ALLAH, desires to give us.

It's not disappointment alone, but the attitude that follows it that demonstrates that our character is either *cursed* or *blessed*.

The Great Jihad

*O*UR great expectations in things and people set us up for even greater 'DISAPPOINTMENTS'. Then, we become angry because *they* are NOT what *we* EXPECT. Have we NO sense?

The World and the People who live in it have never been as we 'THINK' they should be, so why do we expect them to be? This is only to our continual disappointment.

And *this*, is, an example of INSANITY.

I know most people 'THINK' they are not, but yet they only continue to experience frequent disappointment in life, love and our project endeavors.

WHAT makes disappointment so dangerous is that it reveals both the quality and current stage of development of one's heart. Upright is our nature, but we have to be patient while
GOD humbles the proud.

THE womb that spawns hypocrisy is
DISAPPOINTMENT.

Disappointment is what has corrupted most men.

States of Consciousness

PEOPLE that fail you do not simply fail you.

In the broader scope of things, you are the least important person, from where the other person stands, to actually fail. Certainly, our 'egos' may be hurt by disappointment from blind expectations, however, once our 'egos' mature into the Divine, no one will ever be able to hurt us again.

It is an illusion to expect others not to fail in *their* response to OUR predicaments. Our predicaments are our own failures, not the other person we blame.

Learning to do for self is critical to maturity so that we will stop blaming others for the bad things we do to ourselves and others, or for the good things we fail to do for others and ourselves. It's the short-sighted expectations of our 'egos' that puts us at a disadvantage every time and in every relationship.

OUR egos are very fragile by nature.

To be egotistical means that we are being self-centered.

To want for our spouse, child, brother, sister or friend what we want for ourselves is DIVINE.

States of Consciousness

WE must stop trying to teach and advise others out of our anguish and disappointment with what ALLAH has allowed us to endure in life, love and relationships. It may be that ALLAH allowed us to suffer in order to make us more humble for a future use and purpose. If we are always trying to teach others, we MISS OUT on the great lessons that ALLAH sent those individuals into our lives to teach us!

Let's practice LISTENING more, and talking less. Teaching less, and LEARNING more!

The time to teach someone else what you are learning is when you take responsibility for the decisions you have made and find value in your pain and suffering. You are ready to teach others when you STOP seeing yourself as a victim as opposed to a responsible player in the game of life.

The Great Jihad

We reap only what we sow.

Be and do good to ALL, and take not for an intimate partner none save ALLAH, His Messenger and the Believers.

States of Consciousness

Do you think the work of GOD in Creation is done? Creation is still taking place in every instant of time. How can we judge what is still evolving?

We are WARNED against judging others because our thoughts directly affect and influence our individual reality. Justice is like a 'boomerang'. We will always get back what we put out, only it may come from sources we do not expect.

Let's try putting out more LOVE indiscriminately to *all* of creation, and enjoy its many returns!

The Great Jihad

WE are so pridefully 'ignorant' of GOD
that if GOD were the teacher in a classroom,
we would probably 'mistake' Him for one of the students,
and never pay Him any mind.

States of Consciousness

MOST of us like to be in control, and to dictate to others, because the 'god' in us is immature. This is why in the Bible we are called 'children' of the most high GOD. As such, we make many blunders. What do you expect? We are all 'toddlers' in ALLAH's Universe without any
real patience.

The Great Jihad

SOMETIMES, we can become over-critical on how others attribute to ALLAH what trials occur in their lives when we want them to take responsibility for what is happening. ALLAH clearly informs us in the Holy Qur'an that He tries us just on our saying we believe. And severely, at least once a year. Who are we to judge how ALLAH may be working with another person?

Self-mastery, not mastery over others, is our Divine challenge in life. My Father, the Most Honorable Elijah Muhammad, once said that if ALLAH were to leave him for a fraction of a second, in that time you would be looking at a fool.

States of Consciousness

THE ultimate way to handle a 'trial' that we say we believe ALLAH is controlling and that we are seeking refuge in ALLAH from, is to keep it to yourself. DO NOT TALK ABOUT IT with those who are not directly concerned. Your trials are meant for you, sometimes for your immediate family, and nobody else.

So it is with the reward that follows the trial,
if you keep your trust in ALLAH.
It is only for you!

A hypocrite is an emotionally driven person who will always seek to affect others with what negatively affected them.

Beware of this characteristic of the hypocrite so that you might identify it in others and / or yourself.

States of Consciousness

SOME trials we experience in life should be quarantined to prevent contaminating influence in the ear of a sympathizer.

Sympathizers take the misery of others for their own and 'PITY' others' trials. Muslims do not pity others in their trials because they know that nothing happens without ALLAH's permission.

The Great Jihad

THANK ALLAH for your afflictions as they may be a sign that ALLAH desires to purify you for success!

Some of your family members and spouses are adversaries to you, and cause you great pain. It is all permitted by the Unseen GOD, Who intends to make you a better person through the fire of your afflictions. So, thank ALLAH much for not just the Good, but for the trials, pain, and even your enemies in life.

At the end of the day, no matter how trying, you will see by ALLAH . . . IT'S ALL GOOD! Take ALL of your 'issues of complaint' to ALLAH and no one else, with the confidence that He is more than sufficient for us in ALL of our NEEDS.

I cannot react bitterly over others' hatred of me when I LOVE ALLAH with all of my heart, mind and strength.

My love for ALLAH is
my IMMUNITY.

The Great Jihad

FEELING lonely and seemingly being alone
is the final stage before GOD-discovery!

ALLAH demands *exclusivity*.

That is why He waits to make Himself known to us, only
after everything and everyone else has failed us.
In this way, we will each come to bear witness that
THERE IS NO GOD BUT ALLAH!

No one born in this Universe is ever alone.
Whenever we think we are, we are only
temporarily blind.

Healing for Those Who Feel Lost

ALLAH is the All Wise, All Knowing GOD!
He is The Seer,
according to the Holy Qur'an 14:1.

A believer in ALLAH (GOD) does NOT get 'LOST', unless in some way or deed evident in our interpretation of reality, we deviate or disconnect in mind and spirit from HIM (GOD).

Surrender your will to ALLAH.

Seek no possessions, only the pleasure and assistance of ALLAH through PATIENCE and PRAYER, and you will NEVER be 'LOST' again.

The Great Jihad

ANYONE can FACETIME with GOD
on the Spiritual Internet.

The Password is 'PRAYER'.

States of Consciousness

THE final frontier and challenge to our deliverance, individually and as a people, is the overturning of Our INTERNAL government of 'evil' and false-pride, identified as the human 'EGO'.

The Great Jihad

*P*RIDE makes us reactionary.

A prideful person cannot process a critique without becoming bitter.

States of Consciousness

*P*RIDEFUL people are paranoid by nature.
They say and do things in a way to hide
their deficiencies because they do not trust you anymore
than they actually trust their
own dishonest selves.

PRIDE is like the woman that always feels scorned, neglected and unappreciated. This is because PRIDE thinks it is better than what is bothering it.

In truth, ALLAH (GOD) permits us to be bothered so that in humility, we can in fact become better than what we are.

States of Consciousness

ALLAH's Spirit does not flow through prideful people. In fact, when we are emotionally reactionary and are easily given to anger, or any negative emotion, that negative emotion blocks and obstructs our Divinity.

The Great Jihad

We are in a TIME of UNIVERSAL CHANGE!

In this time and age, there can be no successful political, social, economic or religious 'CONSERVATISM'. It is and will continue to be rejected by the populous.
It is not that all conservative ideals are bad, but time itself no longer favors them In their traditional ways. Widespread dissatisfaction among ALL people is calling for CHANGE! Old paradigms have outlived their ability to render FREEDOM, JUSTICE and EQUALITY for the masses.

Time is a force in nature that does not ask, petition or request. IT DEMANDS OF EVERY LIVING CREATURE! Our Beloved Minister Louis Farrakhan teaches us that "Time dictates the agenda!"

COMPROMISING is not necessarily a 'change'
of one's mind or integrity to an ideal.
Being asked to compromise, or in some cases,
having to compromise, means to me
MANAGING and REGULATING
my thinking, ideals and expression
with regard and respect to
another person's
point of view.

Considering another person's view or perspective on anything does not weaken the mind.
Instead, it strengthens and deepens your dimension of thought. An INCONSIDERATE MIND is closed, blind and reckless in its expression. A mind that is unexposed to the diversity of opposing views is a weak mind.
It is opposition, challenges, problems and difficulties that give the Universe itself its creative thrust!
It is what enables it to E X P A N D .

The Great Jihad

SOMETIMES, some people can be so
extremely opposite of the core principles of
the way that we are, that they cause our characters to
suffer incredible ANGER and emotional pain.
Naturally, we want 'them' to change their ways for us.
However, it is ALLAH (GOD),
Who *through* that special someone,
maybe a Parent, Brother, Sister, Spouse,
Son or Daughter . . . is asking *us* to change.

I am grateful to 'ALL MY RELATIONS' for
giving me HELL in order for me to
mature to HEAVEN . . .

States of Consciousness

Dis-Ease & Healing

States of Consciousness

Dis-Ease & Healing

THERE will be difficulty, struggle, opposition, and a tolerable degree of pain in everything we do and undergo in life, whether it is good or bad, right or wrong.

ACCEPT this reality of the process of life itself. Stop looking for ease, comfort and understanding in your woes. There will be none while GOD is trying to use you. Be joyful through afflictions and show GOD that you are grateful to be alive and to be used to serve others!

When we accept the pain and difficulty in the process, in that very moment we will discover ease and great reward, which comes *after* we come through the TRIAL.

Please don't give up or complain while the LORD is your Shepard!

States of Consciousness

*O*UR brains are full of starving 'cells' that cannot properly process water or the nutritional value of any food we eat because it lacks a necessary electrical charge in the cell itself that comes *only from ALLAH.*

Pray to Allah, and BEHOLD!
How He makes ALL Things New . . .
Even YOU!

THE Remembrance of Allah is
The Greatest FORCE!

A mind that is focused on ALLAH,
secretes nutrients to the body that
Revitalize, Repair and *Heal*
any and all infirmity.

The mere idea of ALLAH in the mind
RECREATES and makes all things NEW!

States of Consciousness

WHEN we are neglectful of our prayers, Satan gains the ADVANTAGE! All infirmities and disease are evidence of Satan's occupation in our bodies.

DISHONESTY, FALSE PRIDE, GREED and ENVY are the four leading internal characteristics we must take responsibility for overcoming in order to be healed, saved and delivered from 'evil'.

Dis-Ease & Healing

THE pathological root to all physical infirmities is the aberrated mind. This refers to the mind that has deviated from ALLAH (GOD). The four great fundamental impediments and leading characteristics found in an aberrated person's conditioning are: Dishonesty, False Pride, Greed, and Envy.

States of Consciousness

THE faith of an aberrated mind, by virtue of its deviation in thought from GOD, becomes polytheistic in thinking. When one's worship of GOD becomes polytheistic, they split the power of their own mental focus and weaken the strength of their spiritual energy.

There is only One Universal GOD!

The mere thought of GOD is the greatest organizing principle of healing and repair known to man.

Dis-Ease & Healing

ACCIDENTS are Not COINCIDENCE.
They are the impulsive behaviors of the aberrated mind.
Our state of consciousness determines our
State of BEING.

We must change our internal attitude before ALLAH (GOD) will heal our condition. PRIDE is mental arrogance, fueled by DISAPPOINTMENT, anger and resentment, which can beget CANCER.

Things can always get worse or better depending on our internal attitude and our willingness to change our ways, as we wait on GOD *patiently*.
EVERYTHING is CURABLE.

States of Consciousness

SINCE we ALL have suffered some form or degree of INJUSTICE in our lives, we must NOT think that our bruised egos are capable of proper reasoning from a position of emotional PAIN.
As a believer in GOD, it is a *mercy* available to us to LET GO AND LET GOD!

My Minister taught me that "Every human being must avail him or herself to the MERCY of ALLAH!" Maybe because we are incapable of exacting justice from a standpoint or condition of imbalance.

LET GO AND LET GOD . . .

if you *trust* and *believe* in HIM.

Dis-Ease & Healing

Do not own anger, or let anger own you!
With anger, we will always hurt ourselves
more than those who may actually deserve it.

If it makes sense to you to hate on a sick person,
then that, is how sick, you are.

States of Consciousness

ARE you you ready to punish every violator on the planet? Or just those who cross you? Then pride is your judge! LET GO AND LET GOD!

It may be that GOD wants to teach you something only the HUMBLE can learn.

WORRYING is the misuse of imagination. Stress is default in duty. Control of anything and anyone outside of YOURSELF is but an infantile illusion. Anxiety is a symptom of weakened faith.

If you believe in ALLAH, stop stressing and rushing yourself toward an early grave.

States of Consciousness

WORRYING to a degree is a natural symptom of life, love and faith. The trial that produces our worrying is realizing that we are NOT in control. At best, we can only strive to discipline ourselves in SELF-control of our emotions and how we behave and conduct our affairs, never seeking to control others, depriving them of their Divine Right to FREE-WILL.

"Respect for the rights of others renders PEACE!"
- Benito Juarez -

Dis-Ease & Healing

THE personal challenge we face in all our worries is TRUSTING IN ALLAH!

This was my Parents' greatest example of faith. On my Father's so-called death bed, my Mother worried about our well-being in the eventuality of him not being here. My Father's last words to my Mother were:

"Seek refuge in ALLAH."

For 40 years from February 25th, 1975, to February 16th, 2015, my Mother did just that! She sought refuge in ALLAH through constant prayer, reading of the Holy Qur'an, and following the guidance of the Honorable Minister Louis Farrakhan.

States of Consciousness

WHILE the human being, as a scientist, is born innately curious with intelligence to learn and to discover, when we are believers, our BELIEF relieves us of the stress associated with not knowing . . . because we know that ALLAH is the Best Knower.

"I, Allah, am the best Knower."
~ Holy Qur'an 2:1 ~

Avoid complaining,
as this only contaminates your environment
and diminishes your relationship with GOD.

States of Consciousness

SOMETIMES, when you really listen to people, they sound like they are expressing themselves from mental psychoses. They may not be aware of actual voices in their head because they are impacted and influenced by the exegesis of too many schools of thought. To get acquainted with GOD is the best way to get acquainted with 'self'. So, study the Word Of GOD in both Bible and Holy Qur'an, and guard yourself against polytheism.

Personally, I do not entertain people in the sacred space of my mind who are not GOD-Centered. In this way, I am best able to maintain my mental integrity.

Dis-Ease & Healing

OUR brains possess an organizing component that interprets whatever it reads, listens to, and associates with, relative to 'who' it determines itself to be.

When you know you are created from the infinite Mind of GOD, what you know becomes your potential and no one, is, 'just' anyone.

You are, as you think you are.

States of Consciousness

EVER say 'no' to a compliment.

We know that none of us are good
enough in and of ourselves. Only GOD is Good!
So, what did the other person see, hear and feel from you
that inspired a compliment?

It's the GOD in you!

Accept all compliments and give ALLAH *all* the Praise.
But, NEVER, say 'NO', as this only denies what people are
actually experiencing from you . . . *the beauty of ALLAH.*

Dis-Ease & Healing

OF course you are worthy of a compliment. ALLAH made the whole of His Creation to bow subserviently to you!

The AIR you breath has not stopped complimenting you. The WATER has not stopped complimenting your need for it. You have food, clothing and shelter?

We may not see, hear and feel GOD the way we want to, however, we do have Him always in the manner that we NEED Him!

Now what more do we want? The blind to see you? The deaf to hear you, and the dumb to understand you? We make ourselves LESS than what we are when we wait for others to compliment us.

Isn't it enough that you are here by the permission of ALLAH? Know that you already are somebody because GOD doesn't make junk!

Whenever you feel the need for a compliment, give one to ALLAH through His creatures, and see how He continues to compliment you in ways you do not expect.

States of Consciousness

BEING humble is the best and only way to achieve harmony with ALLAH's Creation.

Dis-Ease & Healing

WHO are you trying to please and get the approval of? If it is anyone other than God, including YOURSELF, it is no wonder that you are so miserable and mediocre in all your affairs and relationships.

Try pleasing ALLAH (GOD/DIOS/The CREATOR)! You have already had His approval since your life began in the womb of your Mother, before she even knew you were there.

States of Consciousness

To live an egotistical life is to live a small life with achievements of diminishing value.

Seek to please ALLAH (GOD/DIOS) in ALL that you do, and you will live a long, happy and prosperous life!

Dis-Ease & Healing

States of Consciousness

Love, Life & Relationships

States of Consciousness

Love, Life & Relationships

LOVE is not what many of us expect.

And, it is generally not what we want.

It is, however,
exactly
what
we NEED.

States of Consciousness

*L*OVE ye one another, even as GOD has already
loved you. GOD does not compliment man in the
manner that we demand it of each other.
Real love, like GOD, tries us by what we want,
while giving us
exactly
what
we
NEED.

Love, Life & Relationships

*L*OVE people not because we deserve it, but because we NEED it! True LOVE is *unlimited*.
We must never withhold it.
It is for ALL from GOD!

States of Consciousness

*L*ooking for LOVE in all the wrong places?
To look for LOVE in all the wrong places is not
a true search for love.

A person who looks for love in all the wrong places does
not actually know love, and in fact confuses love with
fascination of the attracting power of what is
unlike itself.

TO find the 'true' beauty of a WOMAN,
a MAN must seek GOD in her and not be
distracted by her appearance.

GOOD MANNERS displayed enables us to meet GOD in each other.

Good manners access GOD.

Love, Life & Relationships

CIVIL DIALOGUE is a dying artform in today's culture. It is why more than half of our marriages end in divorce, and why our interpersonal fears, differences and conflicts end in violence, death and or destruction of property. This moral downward spiral in people's behaviors indicates that we are in regressive mold, and are co-existing as BEASTS, not humans.

States of Consciousness

THE Holy Qur'an says, "*I, ALLAH, am your only Friend.*"

This means that HE is the Only ONE Worthy of TRUST. On Him we all depend. We are uncongenial partners for one another NOT because we are bad, or necessarily evil. Our humanity, after trillions of years in existence, is still very much in its infancy, which is why the Bible calls us "children of the most High GOD."

Our immaturity disallows our potential to demonstrate greater responsibility for the needs of each other or the exercise of greater LOVE. For this, we must develop our 'spiritual' relationship with *ALLAH,* Who is *Sufficient for us in ALL of our NEEDS.*

Love is the frequency that keeps Believers in ALLAH (GOD) connected.

States of Consciousness

What does it mean to say 'I love you' without affinity?
Affinity is the *evidence of love* between any two people who say 'I love you."

OVE IS 'KIND'.

The above is a Biblical definition of LOVE. I wonder how many of us understand its meaning?
The Scriptures of the Bible tell us of GOD, that
His Thoughts are NOT our thoughts, and
His Ways are NOT our ways.
That being the case, add to the equation our general lack of understanding of the definition of words we use . . .
words of which value we do not really know.

If we do not know the value of a given word, how can we be expected to accurately apply it in attitude or behavior? Please make a moment to study this word, 'KIND', and reflect on how GOD's Love, IS, Kind.

How 'Kind' are WE, to those we say we love?

States of Consciousness

WHEN we expect an aspect of someone's declared love that is KIND, check to see how SIMILAR you are in characteristic to what you seek.

If, as the Bible says, GOD is LOVE, and LOVE is KIND, any wonder how GOD is kind to a people as undeserving of His kindness and unlike His Righteousness as We?
If we would look at ourselves through the eyes of *true humility*, we would know that
GOD's Love and Kindness to us is what is called 'AMAZING GRACE!'

For this reason, ALL PRAISE is due to GOD, and none to any of us.

Love, Life & Relationships

*I*F our love has to be explained, it may be
too heavily infested with PRIDE
to be understood
as LOVE.

PRIDE cripples the charity aspect of LOVE. Pride NEEDS adulation, positive evaluation, praise, and even worship, in order to love. It is no wonder why love is so often misunderstood when PRIDE is its representative.

THE greatest trick our 'pride' makes on us in a relationship with a significant other is when we think we are better than what we attract. Universal Justice dictates that we will all reap what we sow, only we may not know through whom, what, or when what our own deeds committed may come back to revisit us.

In the eyes of ALLAH, none of us are innocent, except those whom He chooses to favor for His Purpose. Even then, ALLAH purifies All through afflictions, especially the PROUD! He does not make anything out of us . . .
until we become
HUMBLE.

We should never think that we are better than what we attract. If you want to change the condition of your relationships, start with YOU.

Love, Life & Relationships

We are no better than the spouse that insecures us, the child that rebels against us, the friends that rebuke and admonish us, those that torment us, or those whose character defects we witness.

When you think you are better than those who bother you, it is only the evil whisperings of that slinking DEVIL, that whispers into the hearts of men from amongst your own kind and from those outside your community you take for friends besides ALLAH, Who is your ONLY TRUE Friend.

WE ARE THE CAUSE of our own reality! You don't like it? Change it within YOURSELF . . . and your environment will follow suit.

States of Consciousness

*Y*OU are as suitable and congenial as a partner, friend, lover, spouse or family member, as your ability to effectively RESPOND to your Own NEEDS without making demands on others to carry your weight under the guise of misinterpreted LOVE.

SOMETIMES, ALLAH puts special people and events in our lives who disagree with our 'way' of thinking or being in order to cause and call us to CHANGE. ALLAH did not make the Male like the Female and call them a 'match'. Un-alike attracts, and cooperation between any two diverse people who strive toward common life goals, aims and values, is a relationship that will remain vibrant and interesting with real staying power!

Tolerating differences is a necessary part of a relationship with the potential of bliss. When we respectfully endure each other, we can become aware that
GOD is the One
Engineering our improvement.

States of Consciousness

EVERY woman needs and deserves a mate (match) of and on her equivalent level of cultural preparation. Mismatching is at the core of many disfunctional relationships.

The Most Honorable Elijah Muhammad said, "You cannot get someone who is MORE intelligent than you to follow you." When women are MORE spiritually sensitive and intellectually advanced than their male counter-parts, men tend to over-accentuate their masculinity, which is our most primitive way of asserting our manhood as an instinct for survival. When a woman is coupled with a man that is insecure within himself, her nature becomes depressed because his handicapped state of being cannot give her, in the relationship, an outlet for full spiritual and intellectual expression.

We must urgently cultivate greater spirituality in our men, which will give birth to a new paradigm and a new world of intelligence from which our women will find greater security and expression. Greater spirituality is greater LOVE, which will make us more sensitive to GOD and allow us to enjoy life more abundantly.

No conscious man can respect a woman who does not share his values and a sense of cultural self-worth. Culture is not history. Culture is our response to environment and our actual communal NEEDS. Any man or woman without a self-sustaining culture is not marriage material. They are unqualified partners who only dream of love but lack the culture to *actually* love and be content.

States of Consciousness

IF we are to produce a 'better' people, believing Women must look for and marry honest, believing Men. Believing Men must look for and marry honest, believing Women. Honest Men must not commit to dishonest women. Honest Women must never subject themselves to dishonest men.

The Honorable Minister Louis Farrakhan once told me that ALL good moral character development starts with the practice of telling the TRUTH.

REAL LOVE seeks to heal, complete, repair, respond and restore. Love has no good utility if and when it is not NEEDED. Loveless relationships, where very little time and attention is given, happens when one or both parties' NEEDS are being met by someone else.

OVE IS CHARITY!

It must be demonstrated without expecting
any reward in return. Love to satisfy a loved one's need!
Love INDISCRIMINATELY, with the selfish aim of purifying
your own heart.

Love is *not* yours to regulate!

Love is channeled *through* you, if your CHARACTER is
found WORTHY to give it as well as to receive it.

ALLAH IS THE SOURCE OF REAL 'LOVE'!

*L*OVE is NOT in a 'place'.
LOVE is an ACTIVITY that *frees, justifies* and makes *equal* two people in a state of perpetual
PEACE and HARMONY
in aim and purpose in life.

States of Consciousness

WHEN we seek things and persons out of our
desires to possess them, including our own lovers and
children, YOU WILL LOSE THEM!
This is because the human being was NOT designed by
ALLAH to hold anything but for so long . . .
not even the life-force itself.

Love, Life & Relationships

RECOGNIZING the HUMAN need for periodic
space and time apart is a matter of life and death.

The less inner activity of mind and spirit of a person,
the less space and time they require apart. As the
Honorable Minister Louis Farrakhan once said in a lecture as
he was describing the living conditions of the 'hood' in the
inner cities where the poor live in project apartments and
houses built so closely together,
"The dead don't need space!"

We all require SPACE and TIME individually, apart,
to GROW.

Most people's ideas about relationships have to be 'unlearned' in order for them to be *enjoyed*.

Love, Life & Relationships

WHEN we look out into space, we may see a cluster of stars that appear to be very close to one another, yet they are really far apart. In our current solar system, there are nine known Planets of various sizes and characteristics. Each has its own proximity to the Sun. Some planets radiate different colors (degrees of light). Some are very large, and others very small.

Based on the activity of each Planet at its core, they all require a considerable measure of SPACE apart from each other. In the nature of every human being exists the NEED for SPACE and TIME apart from each other for continual personal growth and maturation, even for those who are married with multiple children.

States of Consciousness

IF LOVE is truly what any two people experience and feel for one another, it is all they will ever need.

Staying together is NOT the Ultimate AIM of LOVE.

Love is a *creative force*, not a possessive one.

Love is not included as one of the
99 attributes of GOD in Islam.

This is because Love is not an attribute . . .

Love is the CAUSE!

States of Consciousness

A man once asked Prophet Muhammad (PBUH), how he could become of the happiest of men.

The Prophet's response was:
"Be *content*, and you will be of the Happiest of Men."

Love, Life & Relationships

States of Consciousness

God & Religion

States of Consciousness

God & Religion

I am a student of the Holy Qur'an, which means I scientifically observe and experiment with ALLAH's revealed Word in my individual life without IMPOSING it on anyone else, not even on my own children.

ISLAM is a *choice*, NOT a compulsion.

The Way Of ALLAH (GOD) is not compulsory because ALLAH (GOD) respects the 'right' He gives each human being to exercise FREE-WILL. This seems to be the single greatest 'right' most of us grossly violate with each other in our interpersonal relationships.

IF ALLAH (GOD/DIOS/The CREATOR),
Who is the Best Knower, All Wise, Almighty Giver of
Life, will NOT violate the human right to
FREEDOM, JUSTICE and EQUALITY,
then how can we?

WHO are we to judge another man's culture, religion and form of worship? The Holy Qur'an teaches the believer that ALL religions are for ALLAH.

We must never HATE on another man's religion, no matter how different it may be from our own.

Religion is each man's own path to GOD!

God & Religion

*A*LL of us who LOVE the LORD, GOD, ALLAH, & His Prophets are potential ZEALOTS!

LOVE for GOD is never compulsory.

LOVE for GOD comes *naturally*, in TIME.

States of Consciousness

THE world is full of people with diverse perspectives about reality.

All should be respected, but not necessarily followed. Diversity adds dimension to the world that enables us to appreciate what we LIKE and DISLIKE.

My children are from me, but they are not me, or their Mother. Their being 'UNALIKE' makes them very attractive.

Respect for DIVERSITY is the basis for *peace*.

God & Religion

To all of us who love ALLAH:

Was HE not patient and forbearant with us?
As He was to us before we learned to love HIM,
we must be to others!

States of Consciousness

CREATE an atmosphere of LOVE, not LAW.

The 'law' is a fundamental necessity in establishing any and all intra- and inter-personal relationships with family members and society as a whole. Laws are established to be adhered to for the sake of order. Survival in any given domestic culture or society depends on each member developing a degree of personal MORAL DISCIPLINE to respect these laws. Maintenance of the 'laws' that govern anything for a given aim and purpose requires relative personal discipline in being what you want to see.

Laws can be enforced successfully on others with a lasting effect, but NOT without 'LOVE' as the quality and intention of the enforcer of the 'Law!

Remember, LOVE is better *demonstrated* than verbally declared.

God & Religion

WHEN love is talk and not caring
behavior, those who are speaking
become hypocritical to the REAL healing force that
raises the 'Dead' to life and heals the 'sick' . . .
It's all about the LOVE!

Remember, LOVE is better *shown*
than preached.

As Muslims, it is
our MORAL RIGHTEOUSNESS and
the proper 'civil' handling of ALL people that
gives us our IMMUNITY amidst the wiles of this world.

God & Religion

THE Holy Qur'an says that all religions are for Allah. So, the best religion is the one whose members are UPRIGHT in their conduct and behavior.

States of Consciousness

TRY practicing your RELIGION without professing it. You will find that Christian, Muslims and Jews are one! Try loving one another!

God & Religion

THE 'UTOPIA' of GOD is only an idea in the minds of 'Believers', and espoused by religious clergy and some politicians, but it cannot materialize until atmospheric conditions reflect FREEDOM, JUSTICE and EQUALITY for all people regardless of their creed, class, race or color.

Without these atmospheric conditions,
NO righteous society can be established.

States of Consciousness

WHO ARE THE 'MEMBERS' OF THE NATION OF ISLAM?

Because IGNORANCE is so pervasive in the United States of America, I do not consider it a given that people who live in this country know, including many of the rank and file registered members of the Mosques.

According to the teachings of the Most Honorable Elijah Muhammad, ALLAH (GOD) is He Who appeared in the Person of Master FARD MUHAMMAD. The long awaited Messiah of the Christians and Prophesied 'Mahdi' (Self-Guided One) of the Muslims. This is a cardinal belief for all of us who follow the teaching of the Most Honorable Elijah Muhammad and the Honorable Minister Louis Farrakhan.

The Nation of Islam was founded with the coming of GOD our Saviour ALLAH in the Person of Master FARD MUHAMMAD on July 4th, 1930. The membership of the NOI is not limited to those who attend Mosque services. Members of the NOI are all BLACK, NATIVE and INDIGENOUS People of this land who have been victimized and oppressed by European WHITE slave-masters.

All BLACK, BROWN, RED and YELLOW People are members of the Nation of Islam in America regardless of

God & Religion

their creed or class. All BLACK and BROWN members of the various Churches of Christianity are members of the NATION OF ISLAM. This is because ALLAH (GOD) claims them and gives all of our people the title of 'MUSLIM' which means a people surrendered to the Will and Way of GOD. It matters not that anyone agrees or believes with the views of the Nation of Islam. If our claim is true that ALLAH (GOD) actually came in the Person of Master FARD MUHAMMAD, then He intends to bring EVERYTHING into submission to His Will, and no one and nothing can prevent this! He is GOD!

As to 'who' are the members of the Nation of Islam, those that should know are stuck in Mosques, and slow to spread the good news because they think they are the only 'members'. The many who don't know, are stuck in the Church and misguided in the streets of every city of America.

The 'right' to believe or disbelieve comes only after ALL have been INFORMED. This is the duty of the Believers, to inform unbelievers of the Good News of the coming of GOD in the Person of Master FARD MUHAMMAD with the aim of destroying this current wicked and immoral world, and setting-up a UNIVERSAL GOVERNMENT OF PEACE wherein we all will live in true FREEDOM, JUSTICE and EQUALITY.

States of Consciousness

OUR Beloved Minister Farrakhan teaches us that RACISM, CLASSISM and SEXISM are the three main impediments of society. We must fight these 'ISMs' wherever we find them excluding and depriving anyone of FREEDOM, JUSTICE and EQUALITY.

God & Religion

We must PRAY that ALLAH will expand and deepen our personal and collective capacity to LOVE UNCONDITIONALLY.

Where there is NO LOVE demonstrated, there can be NO PEACE.

LOVE is the missing nutrient in all of our lives.

GOD IS LOVE!

TAWHEED: A MUSLIM'S 'KUNG FU'

KUNG FU is popularly understood as a Chinese form of martial arts and self-defense. A deeper study of this term will show that it is much more than a fighting style. KUNG FU is a cultural term that describes an 'art' or 'skill' that is developed through hard work and discipline. Anything a human being does in interaction with others, the perfection of that way necessitates the development of a skill. This is 'KUNG FU'.

The Most Honorable ELIJAH MUHAMMAD taught us that the Chinese People, otherwise identified as the 'Yellow Man', are the Warrior Race. No people or culture should ever be mocked! These are our original people of the Earth. They will play a significant role in our deliverance here in America. My Father said that the Chinese are very wise, even smarter than the 'Jew'.

God & Religion

IN the early 1970's, the Most Honorable Elijah Muhammad was interested in contracting BRUCE LEE to train his followers in Martial Arts. Since then, under the careful guidance of the Honorable Minister Louis Farrakhan, we have had GRAND MASTER DR. MUSA (Moses F. Powell PBUH) and his premier student, GRAND MASTER ANTHONY MUHAMMAD, who serves as our Assistant Supreme Captain of the Nation Of Islam today, training our soldiers in this Divine discipline.

KUNG FU is a Martial Arts form and Divine discipline that is developed as a response to internal and external environmental opposition. ISLAM teaches the Believer in ALLAH from the Holy Qur'an, that ALLAH made 'man' to face difficulty. All life comes into existence fighting. All life must fight to justify its existence. And GOD makes all life rally before He takes it. FIGHTING IS PRESCRIBED BY GOD and must become a mandatory 'skill' developed in EVERY culture. Every culture deserves a Self-Defense.

States of Consciousness

THE original indigenous People of the world tend to be more spiritual than materialistic. So, our resurrection from the material world starts with the cultivation of our spirit. Spiritual development without a conscious aim is like getting 'high' but subject to dangerously subjective negative emotions. For the spiritual and material realms of existence, a Muslims 'Kung Fu' is called in the Arabic language TAWHEED.

TAWHEED means the 'Oness Of ALLAH'. This principle of TAWHEED would imply that there is no force or power outside of ALLAH (GOD) and His Created Uni-verse. Being 'Muslim' is developing the ART and SKILL of acknowledging and praising GOD in everything. This is the acquired 'skill' of a true Muslim . . . to live TAWHEED!

JESUS, the son of Mary, says,
"I am in the Father, and the Father is in me . . . "
This is TAWHEED! When and where GOD is not acknowledged and praised, man become POLYTHEISTIC. TAWHEED is the greatest KUNG FU for the Believer on the straight 'Path' to becoming One with GOD!

God & Religion

We simply cannot grow into the beings ALLAH intends for us to become if we are not more responsible in our roles to build, maintain, sustain and preserve the longevity of the environmental peace and righteousness we want to see.

A Muslim is one who obeys, follows and respects ANY authority over them so long as it does not CONFLICT with our religion. No ranking official or authority figure, including a parent or a spouse, has the right to violate and disrespect your GOD-given right to Freedom, Justice and Equality to pursue the full measure of your unique individuality and expression to the degree that it does not hinder others in their right to be themselves.

Wherever you may feel and experience any degree of injustice and unfair treatment, STOP BEING SILENT COWARDS and verbal hypocrites! If you are being mistreated, disrespected, ignored and mishandled, JUSTICE is just an ACT of COURAGE AWAY!

States of Consciousness

COWARDS who fail to act become silent accomplices to the crimes of those in authority over them. Cowards enable tyrants.

Every Man and Woman, as an authority figure, operates under the authority of another, and ALL operate under the Authority and Permission of ALLAH (GOD / DIOS)! Men fear men as they ought to fear ALLAH!

God & Religion

WHEN we idolize something or someone, we arrest our own growth & development.

A Muslim must be very careful NOT to praise ANYONE beside ALLAH the Most High.

States of Consciousness

THE human being is always in NEED of ALLAH's guidance. When we 'idolize' something or someone, we arrest our own growth and development.

In ISLAM, when a person makes their transition, during their Jenazah (Prayer Service for those who pass on), there is no 'eulogy' because in this word is the attribute of praise, and all praise is due to ALLAH (GOD). A Muslim must be very careful NOT to praise ANYONE beside ALLAH, the Most High.

When we discipline our focus on ALLAH, we will find that He has given us many examples, starting with our own nearest of kin, by whom we can learn all about ourselves.

God & Religion

OUR belief in ALLAH as the Best Knower does NOT exempt us from study, research and investigation. In fact, the very first revelation that Prophet Muhammad (PBUH) received was to "READ"!

KNOWLEDGE must be 'studied',
and not carelessly assumed.

KNOWLEDGE can be dangerous when
in the possession of irresponsible, wicked, undisciplined,
disrespectful and evil-minded people.

KNOWLEDGE must never be used to
oppress, suppress or repress another who is likewise born
with the universal right to
FREEDOM, JUSTICE and EQUALITY
regardless of their creed, class, race or color.

KNOWLEDGE is a human right to have and acquire.
KNOWLEDGE must be a societal requirement.
KNOWLEDGE is a 'human' right of passage to
freedom, justice and equality.

When you have KNOWLEDGE, you know you are FREE!

God & Religion

KNOWLEDGE makes a person 'functional'.
The absence of knowledge makes men and women
SAVAGES driven only by their lower desires.
KNOWLEDGE is what distinguishes
'Man' from animals and beasts.

KNOWLEDGE makes a person want to do things as
opposed to just acquiring them.
KNOWLEDGE does not want to rest.
It desires to build and be active.

KNOWLEDGE of GOD is prerequisite knowledge.
It is why a knowledge of GOD THROUGH ALL OF
THE NATURAL SCIENCES is a must study.

Knowledge is awareness.
Man cannot navigate successfully without KNOWLEDGE!

The real thing we should ALL study is... EVERYTHING :-)

IGNORANCE is a state of mind that habitually ignores critical realities and/or Truth.

CONFUSION is disorder of the mind and its thinking. Extraordinary atmospheric stress is the current main cause for the 'stupidity' (dulling of the senses) exhibited by most people today.

Our immoral lifestyles have brought us to this Day of Requital. We are ALL being terrorized by the consequences of our own wicked deeds. No one is exempt.

It is ALLAH (GOD) Who is Judging us today.

God & Religion

A 'DIS-believer' is not one without knowledge. A 'DIS-believer' is a REJECTOR of the Messages of the Messenger that comes to the people out of the Grace and Mercy of ALLAH so that we all have a chance to be saved in the 'Rapture'.

A 'DIS-believer' is angry at GOD for the trials He permits in their life.

A 'DIS-believer's' life journey is on the path of those upon whom the wrath of ALLAH is brought down.

States of Consciousness

A 'Dis-believer' is the natural enemy of your faith. ALLAH forbids our association with them. When Believers take 'DIS-believers' for friends, your love for them, even if they happen to be blood-relatives, will eventually turn you out of your faith. A Believer's lack of success is often due to their association with 'DIS-believers' and hypocrites. They rob you of your Reward.

God & Religion

CRITICAL analysis, which seems to be the culture of contemporary liberal intelligence, leads to dangerous judgment without regard for GOD.

CRITICAL ANALYSIS without regard for GOD is the thinking of an ATHEIST that compromises 'FAITH' in ALLAH (GOD) because we think we know. When we think we know, we tend to pass judgment.

Hypocrites are devils who are critical beneath the notion that they are your friends. The nature of a hypocrite is that they are HYPO- (beneath or undercover) CRITICAL. Hypocrites are almost completely unaware of themselves because they THINK they know and they JUDGE. Most hypocrites think of themselves as repositories of special knowledge and wisdom that nobody else has.

States of Consciousness

A HYPOCRITE does NOT believe that ALLAH (GOD) is in CONTROL of people and occurrences. So they seek to be in control of the public opinion concerning individuals they feel threatened by or in competition with.

Even though the Holy Qur'an says that NOTHING happens without ALLAH's Permission, a HYPOCRITE does NOT believe this. They do NOT believe that ALLAH is LORD (GOVERNOR) of ALL the worlds, and they judge in the place of ALLAH (GOD).

God & Religion

HYPOCRITES are natural CONSPIRATORS bent on the demise of the personality whose life-activity obstructs or interferes with their aim. They are deeply disturbed individuals who hate on anyone whose SUCCESS threatens their delusional sense of worth, and because they judge others in the place of GOD.

The disease in the heart of a hypocrite is 'ENVY'.

States of Consciousness

A HYPOCRITE is most effective from a position of INFLUENCE. Like a spouse, family member, close trusted confidant, high or low ranking official with sway over the thinking of the followers of the 'MARK'. A HYPOCRITE / CONSPIRATOR is a chameleon, they operate under the cover of your 'friend'.

As a protection to the Believer who cannot identify the HYPOCRITE who is part of the CONSPIRACY bent on their demise, the Holy Qur'an tells us that ALLAH (GOD) is our ONLY 'FRIEND'. If, as a Believer, you believe this, then you are secure in your faith by YOUR trust in ALLAH!
No weapon formed against you will prosper.
You are immune by your FAITH in ALLAH!

God & Religion

To the Delusional Paranoid 'BELIEVER' who
lives in fear and is always thinking that
powerful entities are out to get them . . .
RELAX.

Inactivity does NOT inspire opposition.
We have only the enemies we produce by the
ACTIVITY of what we claim to believe.

PEOPLE tend to fear the likeness or
probability of the WRONG-DOING they themselves
have done or are currently doing to others. They attack
and falsely accuse you in an effort to keep
the attention off of themselves.

God & Religion

States of Consciousness

The Time

States of Consciousness

The Time

TODAY'S technological culture puts all of us and our expressions on the world stage!

Please, let us mind our MANNERS.

States of Consciousness

TO 'MODERATE' means to keep something from an extreme. Whether we are moderating a public forum or our personal lives, we should always guard against extremes. The technical term in religion for exceeding the limits of GOD's Law is considered 'evil'. To exceed the limits in anything is to lose control.

The Holy Qur'an teaches 'moderation' in the following verse: "Mild obedience is all that is required." There is NO extremism in Islam. ALLAH is the great Universal Moderator Who says nothing happens without His Permission! This is because He is in CONTROL of everything and everyone, including the 'Devil'.

To be 'moderate' politically, religiously and in our personal views demonstrates great self-control, respect and civility toward others whether at home, in the work place or elsewhere in public.

LOVE makes the best 'Moderator'.
LOVE gives balance to everything.

WHO Should Be Worried Today?

If you believe in ALLAH (GOD / DIOS / The CREATOR) which means that you are aware that we are NOW living in the time of His JUDGMENT of this World that we live in, and every one of us, regardless of our religious declarations, are individually under judgment.

RAIN, HAIL, SNOW and EARTHQUAKES in diverse places, meaning where they are NOT usually expected, are all the atmospheric conditions by which ALLAH (GOD) will Judge. By upsetting things we all think of as 'normal', even to what we think we are moral and intellectual authorities in will be challenged by circumstances beyond our control. There is NO defense against the Judgement Of GOD.

While in a time of ALLAH's Judgment of us ALL, it is critical to those of us who are 'Believers' to remain HUMBLE in mind, attitude and behavior. Arrogance will actually trigger the atmospheric wrath Of GOD upon you and your loved ones as retribution for what your deeds have caused.

States of Consciousness

THE real devil today is the one who appeals to your pain and dissatisfaction, and fakes concern for you in your trials to gain your trust. English Lesson #C1 tells us that the devil can get amongst us as a 'Trader', but he is really a TRAITOR making an interpretation that what they offer will make you wiser than the teaching you have already received as 'Supreme Wisdom' from the Most Honorable Elijah Muhammad and His Representative the Honorable Minister Louis Farrakhan, and will soon discover that your hearts and wicked associations have BETRAYED you. When they disappear, the betrayed will NOT be able to remember the original teaching that first raised them from the 'dead'.

Seek assistance from ALLAH through PATIENCE and PRAYER, for and from an attitude of great HUMILITY. Only the guilty, proud and disappointed disbeliever and hypocrite should be very worried today.
They have no hope in ALLAH.

The Time

BIGOTRY is a symptom of the misguided notion of inordinate self, class, race or color superiority. Bigotry begets racism, sexism, classism, intellectual, moral and religious ORTHODOXY. This degree of immaturity must never be allowed into positions of leadership in a culturally diverse world. FREEDOM, JUSTICE and EQUALITY are meant for ALL, regardless of creed, class, race or color.

There is a degree of bigotry found in every sphere of leadership in the world, exclusive to none, as a means by which immaturity attempts to preserve and protect its concept of values against the perceived threat of powerful influential 'change'.

At this time in history, NO ONE should be a 'conservative' if we hope for a better tomorrow. Whoever and wherever you are in the world, I challenge you to be an 'ACTIVIST' for Freedom, Justice and Equality,
in *everything*,
for *everyone*.

This is an essential step in the direction and aim of setting up a Universal Government of PEACE.

States of Consciousness

We are all under trial from GOD, regardless of creed, class, race or color. He's trying us because He wants to use us and make us *worthy*.

The Time

WHEN leadership lacks good moral character, everyone that follows is going straight to hell.

States of Consciousness

DEEP within many of us is FEAR . . Fear of the REALITY of GOD. It is easy to believe in the representation of GOD in the past. Mainstream religion is based on this false interpretation of the 'transcending' and 'translucent' appearance of the reality of GOD.

Our faith and declared belief in ALLAH (GOD) is not challenged if our doctrines remain archaic in its interpretation, which is the case when and if your religious teachers spend too much time preaching about GOD in the past-tense as opposed to showing the revelatory presence of GOD in the NOW and relative to us in our times.

Our school of of thought in the Nation Of Islam is rooted in the belief that ALLAH (GOD) when intervening in the affairs of human beings, appears in the Person of One. Were we other than human beings, then GOD could be expected to appear in another form relative to us.

The Time

THE 'Apocalyptic' end of this world is very near! Even though we know Scripturally that none knows the precise moment when it will all be over, the Believer and the intense student of history have and can intuitively predict the period and read the signs.

NO ARROGANT DISBELIEVER WILL SURVIVE THE 'APOCALYPSE' OR WAR OF ARMAGEDDON! Disbelief is suicide in the time of ALLAH (GOD) executing His Will in delivering a people from mental and spiritual bondage and the setting up of His Universal Government of PEACE.

THE BELIEVERS are not simply the ones who declare their belief in ALLAH (GOD) with their tongues. The BELIEVER are those who LOVE what ALLAH LOVES, which is RIGHTEOUSNESS in thought and behavior. The BELIEVER is aware of ALLAH's Judgement and the 'Last Day'. We must NEVER be proud and strive hard to be HUMBLE. Humility is the hallmark of a believer.

ALLAH through the Honorable Minister Louis Farrakhan's MINISTRY OF LOVE, is a MERCY to all the Mosques and Study Groups who have tried to follow the teachings and live them. ALLAH always sends MERCY before the end.

States of Consciousness

THE battlefield of the War of Armageddon is the human HEART. Love is the greatest weapon. If you're armed with LOVE, you have nothing to fear!

The Time

NOT just any love will conquer all . . .

But GOD's Love will!

States of Consciousness

We are in very dangerous days where we do not know with certainty the very next moment, whether we will live or die. We do not know if yesterday's friend will in fact still be that today. However, regardless of what comes or goes in your life, keep evolving yourself into a more and more righteous being by the doing of 'Good' by all people regardless of their creed, class, race or color.

Did you know that the doing of good by each other is in fact an investment in self? Yes, this how you bless yourself . . . It is by *blessing others*.

The Time

I woke up this morning at a little past 3:10am and said several prayers before making a pot of my Mom's egg-coffee for the Minister. As I knew he had an early flight to catch, I wanted him to at least get a cup of coffee down with the 'RaRa' touch. :-) As he sipped his coffee we began reflecting on my Mom (Mother Tynnetta) with great words of HOPE. When it was time to go the Minister said to me joyfully as if he were in the future speaking back to me in present time..

"Ra! We're going to be ALRIGHT!"

With that I kissed and hugged my Minister as he departed.

As I went back in the house after watching him pull off, I broke down and cried because I feel like I've come to know his heart of LOVE.. and my feeling of never being and doing enough to help him and because it feels horrible to watch someone you LOVE leave anywhere without you.. And maybe simply because I just LOVE MINISTER FARRAKHAN WITH MY WHOLE HEART.

Well, I'm sharing this with all of you and especially the BELIEVERS; as the Messenger of ALLAH blessed my life this morning I am hoping to bless yours with his words to me:
"WE'RE GOING TO BE ALRIGHT!"

States of Consciousness

Concluding Thoughts on Love

States of Consciousness

Concluding Thoughts

LOVE is Kind, LOVE is Patient.

LOVE is NOT weak, LOVE is STRONG!

If we practiced this as behavior indiscriminately, we would improve our relationships, advance our 'culture' and *transfigure* our 'character' INSTANTANEOUSLY!

KINDNESS is an act that is to wrongful behavior as water is to fire, particularly when the nature of the wrong doer is righteous.

Concluding Thoughts

KINDNESS may seem like a simple act,
but when it carries the power of INTENTION, it carries
within it the medicinal power of the DIVINE.
If your act of kindness proves ineffective, it may be that it
lacked the power of Kind Intention, so it never even
reached your target.

BE KIND, and let the *healing* in all your
interpersonal relationships begin . . .

States of Consciousness

IN most instances, conflict resolution requires an 'act' of KINDNESS, not just 'words' of apology. Especially from those who 'think' they've done nothing wrong. If you are 'innocent', you are in the best position to bear some responsibility in the interest of
LOVE and PEACE.

Your brother, sister, lover, friend . . . she or he ain't heavy. 'They' are only as heavy as you are weak in LOVE.

Concluding Thoughts

THE POWER OF KINDNESS

The nature of black and indigenous people is righteousness. By nature, we are spiritually, mentally and morally inclined to do everything right. This means that whenever we do something wrong, we are merely acting other than our true selves.

The Arabic word 'Jinn' describes the fiery nature of and in the human being, regardless of their creed, class, race or color. While the 'Jinn' is not the nature of black and indigenous people, it is a part of our nature, which gives us the capacity to be prideful, arrogant, temperamental and even evil.

We are designed by nature to obey GOD! Our culture is the culture of GOD! Any of us indoctrinated in the Western European Culture of Caucasians in religion, education and civilization suffer an aberrated mind as a direct result. We have been morally tricked and intellectually crippled to believe that the culture of white people is ours . . . It is not.

States of Consciousness

WHEN you see a black or indigenous person behaving other than themselves, KINDNESS is the antidote that will repair their aberrated state of mind, meaning the mind and its rationale that has deviated from the Divine. This is why I assert that kindness to Black and Indigenous people is as water to fire.

Remember, any wrongful behavior or evil committed by Black and Indigenous people is FORGIVABLE. It can be atoned for because of its fundamental nature in the power of it's being, which is RIGHTEOUSNESS.

Concluding Thoughts

We are a people totally destroyed in the requisite knowledge of self and our natural, spiritual and moral connection to GOD. The Bible refers to GOD as LOVE, but to comprehend this Biblical concept we must not think of 'Love' as being limited to an emotion. Love is much more than an emotion! LOVE is a creative force that is activated and inspired by human suffering and needs.

To think of GOD as an emotion is to say He is moved to Love as we are, which is a very low level of Love that dismisses the creative essence of it, and thus, makes it REACTIONARY. GOD's Love is PROACTIVE, and critical, because it seeks to fix, repair, restore, cure, heal and advance all life. It is the misconception of our egos about Love that demands compliments and approval.

GOD does not cater to the perceived needs of our egos, and neither do the people in our lives who truly Love us.

States of Consciousness

WHY is it that ALLAH (GOD) is oft returning to MERCY AND FORGIVENESS?

The short answer is because He is Pure LOVE. There are no conditions in us that can alter His LOVE. And We are capable of loving each other the same way . . . It's called UNCONDITIONAL LOVE!

Concluding Thoughts

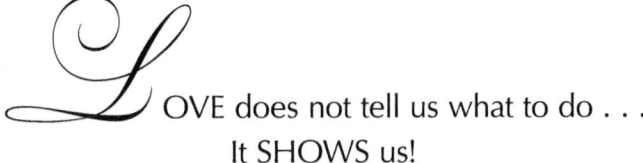OVE does not tell us what to do . . .
It SHOWS us!

The language we use as Spouses, Parents,
Religious Officials, and Authority Figures, is NOT Love.
This is why harmony, if achieved, is short lived . . .
LOVE'S AUTHORITY does not dictate.

It *suggests*.

LOVE is the Way of GOD.

GOD shows compassion for all of His creatures. And none is closer in potential to ALLAH than the Human Being. Let us, through 'kindness' and 'patience', learn to speak the language that appeals to the GOD within each other to achieve what we want. That's LOVE!

States of Consciousness

Epilogue

States of Consciousness

EPILOGUE

The following words shared by Brother Rasul on the birth anniversary of Our Saviour, Master Fard Muhammad, on Februay 26, 2016, offer a glimpse into the ultimate goal and aim of the inner workings of the mind that produced the reflections contained in this volume.

I am attempting to purify the INNER SANCTUM of my mind of all transgressional thoughts that offend GOD.

I MUST create an electromagnetic force by the quality of my thinking and the righteousness of my lifestyle in order to expel spiritual wickedness and immoral influences. I must develop the inner atmosphere of my mind to make it fit for ALLAH to appear in my person. My intention is NOT to be saved, but to be USED by ALLAH (GOD / DIOS) for His Purpose to heal and improve the human condition.

I'm learning how to activate my 'Soul', the Divine core of my being. This is where the electro-magnetic force is produced that will protect me from deadly viruses and negative forces carried by people, the air we breath, and the water we drink,

Epilogue

just as our planet protects itself from most deadly asteroids and space objects that are on a collision couse with it. I'm learning how to both cure and strengthen my own immune system so that ALLAH may make greater use of me in this world before I evolve out of view.

As the human brain is a chemical factory for the body, I expect that soon I will be able to produce from my mind by a single purified thought the right chemical cure for the healing of my body organs. I'm NOT dying . . . I'm on a cellular level in the process of my own transfiguration into a more suitable form for my Divine mission in life, which is to heal people. I could not have ever discovered this great power to LOVE and HEAL people if I had not fallen sick myself.

We are ALL born of very advanced material far ahead of this current time, which is why ALLAH requires of us all patience, humility and endurance while He continues to Pave the Way.

States of Consciousness

ACKNOWLEDGEMENTS

Special thanks to the Honorable Minister Louis Farrakhan and Mother Khadijah Farrakhan for their encouragement and constant support of me. Also, special thanks to Mustapha and Karen Farrakhan, my sister Madeeah Bey Muhammad, my brothers Ishmael R. Muhammad and Ahmad F. Muhammad, and my daughters Jamillah and Amani Muhammad for always providing love and inspiration for everything I do.

A special thank you to my assistant, Sabrina F. Muhammad, and the entire staff of G.C. Productions. Also, thank you to my wonderful family on the Live Chat.

www.ingramcontent.com/pod-product-compliance
Lightning Source LLC
Chambersburg PA
CBHW071434150426
43191CB00008B/1126